Sharing Love Series 2015

Sharing Love Series 2015

James Edward Hyler II

ISBN: 1517391199
ISBN 13: 9781517391195
Library of Congress Control Number: 2015915664
CreateSpace Independent Publishing Platform
North Charleston, South Carolina

Sharing Love Sprouts

Dormant in earth.
Nine months in crack.
Rain gushes out.
Sharing Love sprouts.

Leaves not normal—
misshapen, mashed.
Nine months of growth;
all leaves normal.

Sharing Love's Knothole

Dormant in winter.
Felt a big bone snake
entering knothole.
Will call my Angel.

Sharing Love dialed 777-7777.
Phone began to ring.
Angel began to sing,
"Hello, may I help you?"

"Felt a big bone snake
entering knothole."
Angel killed bone snake,
hung on tree for rain.

Sharing Love Saves Drunk

Dormant in winter.
Snow covering ground.
Felt truck hit trunk,
wrapped all around.

Sharing Love dialed 777-7777.
Phone began to ring.
Angel began to sing,
"Hello, may I help you?"

"Felt truck hit trunk,
wrapped all around."
Angel called 911.
Man alive found.

Sharing Love Finds Appleseed

Alive in spring.
Sap rising.
Games played by all
with Angel.

Sharing Love dialed 777-7777.
Phone began to ring.
Angel began to sing,
"Hello, may I help you?"

"Play Appleseed game.
Sounds like lots of fun."
Appleseed hid in wet, warm crack.
Fastest time wins, retrieving back.

Sharing Love Attacked

Sleepy in fall.
Sap was draining.
Trunk under attack—
illegal logger.

Sharing Love dialed 777-7777.
Phone began to ring.
Angel began to sing,
"Hello, may I help you?"

"Trunk under attack—
illegal logger."
Angel called park ranger.
Logger no longer back.

Sharing Love's Broken Limb

Growing in summer.
Bad storm arriving.
Limb broken—
am dying.

Sharing Love dialed 777-7777.
Phone began to ring.
Angel began to sing,
"Hello, may I help you?"

"Limb broken—
am dying."
Angel got tree doctor.
Sharing Love surviving.

Sharing Love Breaks Glass

Sleepy in fall.
Fruit was falling.
Lands on grass ground.
Breaks picnic glass.

Sharing Love dialed 777-7777.
Phone began to ring.
Angel began to sing,
"Hello, may I help you?"

"Fruit was falling.
Broke picnic glass."
Angel cleaned up glass.
Grass on ground safe at last.

Sharing Love Befriends Redhead

Flowering in spring.
Felt sharp needle thing
drilling holes
in dead branch.

Sharing Love dialed 777-7777.
Phone began to ring.
Angel began to sing,
"Hello, may I help you?"

"Felt sharp needle thing
in me drilling holes."
"Just friend—redheaded woodpecker,
deworming your dead branches."

Sharing Love Cracks Limb

Sunny March day.
Kites in windy play.
Felt limb crack.
Pain down trunk back.

Sharing Love called 777-7777.
Phone began to ring.
Angel began to sing,
"Hello, may I help you?"

"Felt limb crack.
Pain down trunk back."
Angel got tree doctor.
Pain went quickly slack.

Sharing Love Feels AC/DC

Summertime in air.
Picnics everywhere.
Felt thump, thump
in trunk, trunk.

Sharing Love dialed 777-7777.
Phone began to ring.
Angel began to sing,
"Hello, may I help you?"

"Felt thump, thump
in trunk, trunk."
"Just band AC/DC—
'Highway to Hell.'"

Sharing Love Feels Alison Krauss

Summertime in air.
Picnics everywhere.
Felt thump, thump
in trunk, trunk.

Sharing love dialed 777-7777.
Phone began to ring.
Angel began to sing,
"Hello, may I help you?"

"Felt thump, thump
in trunk, trunk."
"Just singer Alison Krauss—
'Down to the River to Pray.'"

Sharing Love Feels Otis Redding

Summertime in air.
Picnics everywhere.
Felt thump, thump
in trunk, trunk.

Sharing Love dialed 777-7777.
Phone began to ring.
Angel began to sing,
"Hello, may I help you?"

"Felt thump, thump
in trunk, trunk."
"Just soul singer Otis Redding—
'(Sittin' on) the Dock of the Bay.'"

Sharing Love Feels Casting Crowns

Summertime in air.
Picnics everywhere.
Felt thump, thump
in trunk, trunk.

Sharing Love dialed 777-7777.
Phone began to ring.
Angel began to sing,
"Hello, may I help you?"

"Felt thump, thump
in trunk, trunk."
"Just Christian band Casting Crowns—
'Does Anybody Hear Her?'"

Sharing Love Feels ELO

Springtime in air.
Picnics everywhere.
Felt thump, thump
in trunk, trunk.

Sharing Love dialed 777-7777.
Phone began to ring.
Angel began to sing,
"Hello, may I help you?"

"Felt thump, thump
in trunk, trunk."
"Band ELO—
'Telephone Line.'"

Sharing Love Hears George Washington

Summertime breezing.
White man just sneezing,
using trunk
as a stump.

Sharing Love dialed 777-7777.
Phone began to ring.
Angel began to sing,
"Hello, may I help you?"

"Using trunk
as a stump."
"Just George Washington—
political speech."

Sharing Love Hears Abe Lincoln

Summertime breezing.
White man just sneezing,
using trunk
as a stump.

Sharing Love dialed 777-7777.
Phone began to ring.
Angel began to sing,
"Hello, may I help you?"

"Using trunk
as a stump."
"Just old Abe Lincoln—
political speech."

Sharing Love Hears Richard Nixon

Summertime breezing.
White man just sneezing,
using trunk
as a stump.

Sharing Love dialed 777-7777.
Phone began to ring.
Angel began to sing,
"Hello, may I help you?"

"Using trunk
as a stump."
"Just Richard Nixon—
political speech."

Sharing Love Hears Barack Obama

Summertime breezing.
Black man just sneezing,
using trunk
as a stump.

Sharing Love dialed 777-7777.
Phone began to ring.
Angel began to sing,
"Hello, may I help you?"

"Using trunk
as a stump."
"Just Barack Obama—
political speech."

Sharing Love Hears Hillary Clinton

Summertime breezing.
White woman sneezing,
using trunk
as a stump.

Sharing Love dialed 777-7777.
Phone began to ring.
Angel began to sing,
"Hello, may I help you?"

"Using trunk
as a stump."
"Just Hillary Clinton—
political speech."

Sharing Love Bumps Marilyn Monroe

Wintertime snow.
Lights shine aglow.
Bumpily bumping,
my trunk now barking.

Sharing Love dialed 777-7777.
Phone began to ring.
Angel began to sing,
"Hello, may I help you?"

"Bumpily bumping,
my trunk now barking."
"Just Marilyn Monroe—
singing 'Diamonds Are a Girl's Best Friend.'"

Sharing Love Bumps Elvis Presley

Wintertime snow.
Lights shine aglow.
Bumpily bumping,
my trunk now barking.

Sharing Love dialed 777-7777.
Phone began to ring.
Angel began to sing,
"Hello, may I help you?"

"Bumpily bumping,
my trunk now barking."
"Just Elvis Presley-
'singing Hound Dog.'"

Sharing Love Bumps Tina Turner

Wintertime snow.
Lights shine aglow.
Bumpily bumping,
my trunk now barking.

Sharing Love dialed 777-7777.
Phone began to ring.
Angel began to sing,
"Hello, may I help you?"

"Bumpily bumping
my trunk now barking."
"Just Tina Turner-
singing 'Respect.'"

Sharing Love Bumps Nat King Cole

Wintertime snow.
Lights shine aglow.
Bumpily bumping,
my trunk now barking.

Sharing Love dialed 777-7777.
Phone began to ring.
Angel began to sing,
"Hello, may I help you?"

"Bumpily bumping,
my trunk now barking."
"Just Nat King Cole-
singing 'Unforgettable.'"

Sharing Love Bumps Britney Spears

Wintertime snow.
Lights shine aglow.
Bumpily bumping,
my trunk now barking.

Sharing Love dialed 777-7777.
Phone began to ring.
Angel began to sing,
"Hello, may I help you?"

"Bumpily bumping,
my trunk now barking."
"Just friend Britney Spears—
singing '(You Drive Me) Crazy.'"

Sharing Love Breathes Tom Hanks

Fall leaves falling.
Popcorn popping.
Some leaf tears flowed
down trunk spilled.

Sharing Love dialed 777-7777.
Phone began to ring.
Angel began to sing,
"Hello, may I help you?"

"Some leaf tears flowed
down trunk spilled."
"Tom Hanks—
movie Forrest Gump."

Sharing Love Breathes Vivien Leigh

Fall leaves falling.
Popcorn popping.
Some leaf tears flowed
down trunk spilled.

Sharing Love dialed 777-7777.
Phone began to ring.
Angel began to sing,
"Hello, may I help you?"

"Some leaf tears flowed
down trunk spilled."
"Vivien Leigh—
movie Gone with the Wind."

Sharing Love Breathes Albert Finney

Fall leaves falling.
Popcorn popping.
Some leaf tears flowed
down trunk spilled.

Sharing Love dialed 777-7777.
Phone began to ring.
Angel began to sing,
"Hello, may I help you?"

"Some leaf tears flowed
down trunk spilled."
"Albert Finney
movie *Big Fish*."

Sharing Love Breathes Rachel McAdams

Fall leaves falling.
Popcorn popping.
Some leaf tears flowed
down trunk spilled.

Sharing Love dialed 777-7777.
Phone began to ring.
Angel began to sing,
"Hello, may I help you?"

"Some leaf tears flowed
down trunk spilled."
"Rachel McAdams
movie *The Notebook*."

Sharing Love Breathes Jimmy Stewart

Fall leaves falling.
Popcorn popping.
Some leaf tears flowed
down trunk spilled.

Sharing Love dialed 777-7777.
Phone began to ring.
Angel began to sing,
"Hello, may I help you?"

"Some leaf tears flowed
down trunk spilled."
"Jimmy Stewart—
movie It's a Wonderful Life."

Sharing Love Feels Nolan Ryan

Summertime circles;
earth playing abounds.
Felt bump
on trunk.

Sharing Love dialed 777-7777.
Phone began to ring.
Angel began to sing,
"Hello, may I help you?"

"Felt bump
on trunk."
"Playing baseball—
Nolan Ryan."

Sharing Love Feels Michael Jordan

Wintertime circles;
earth playing abounds.
Felt bump
on trunk.

Sharing Love dialed 777-7777.
Phone began to ring.
Angel began to sing,
"Hello, may I help you?"

"Felt bump
on trunk."
"Playing basketball—
Michael Jordan."

Sharing Love Feels Fran Tarkenton

Falltime circles;
earth playing abounds.
Felt bump
on trunk.

Sharing Love dialed 777-7777.
Phone began to ring.
Angel began to sing,
"Hello, may I help you?"

"Felt bump
on trunk."
"Playing football—
Fran Tarkenton."

Sharing Love Feels Hulk Hogan

Summertime circles;
earth playing abounds.
Felt bump
on trunk.

Sharing Love dialed 777-7777.
Phone began to ring.
Angel began to sing,
"Hello, may I help you?"

"Felt bump
on trunk."
"Playing wrestling—
Hulk Hogan."

Sharing Love Feels Dale Earnhardt

Summertime circles;
earth playing abounds.
Felt bump
on trunk.

Sharing Love dialed 777-7777.
Phone began to ring.
Angel began to sing,
"Hello, may I help you?"

"Felt bump
on trunk."
"Playing racing—
Dale Earnhardt."

Sharing Love Tastes McDonald's

Winter smells in air.
Earth hunger everywhere.
Tasted food
in my roots.

Sharing Love dialed 777-7777.
Phone began to ring.
Angel began to sing,
"Hello, may I help you?"

"Tasted food
in my roots."
"Tasted McDonald's—
Big Mac."

Sharing Love Tastes Wendy's

Winter smells in air.
Earth hunger everywhere.
Tasted food
in my roots.

Sharing Love dialed 777-7777.
Phone began to ring.
Angel began to sing,
"Hello, may I help you?"

"Tasted food
in my roots."
"Tasted Wendy's
Hamburger."

Sharing Love Tastes Burger King

Winter smells in air.
Earth hunger everywhere.
Tasted food
in my roots.

Sharing Love dialed 777-7777.
Phone began to ring.
Angel began to sing,
"Hello, may I help you?"

"Tasted food
in my roots."
"Tasted Burger King
Whopper."

Sharing Love Tastes Arby's

Winter smells in air.
Earth hunger everywhere.
Tasted food
in my roots.

Sharing Love dialed 777-7777.
Phone began to ring.
Angel began to sing,
"Hello, may I help you?"

"Tasted food
in my roots."
"Tasted Arby's
Roast Beef."

Sharing Love Tastes Chick-fil-A

Winter smells in air.
Earth hunger everywhere
Tasted food
in my roots.

Sharing Love dialed 777-7777.
Phone began to ring.
Angel began to sing,
"Hello, may I help you?"

"Tasted food
in my roots."
"Tasted Chick-fil-A
Chicken Sandwich."

Sharing Love Thanks Angel

Springs pass.
Falls pass.
Summers pass.
Winters pass.

Sharing Love dialed 777-7777.
Phone began to ring.
Angel began to sing,
"Hello, may I help you?"

"Apples are red.
Branches are blue.
Want to thank you,
say 'I love you.'"

About the Author

James E. Hyler II is a Virginia native who currently resides in the town of Monroe.

He starts each day by feeding the birds and going for an hour-long walk. Hyler is a prolific poet who has had much success publishing his work on www.allpoetry.com and enjoys reading new poems on the website each day.

He is the proud father of one daughter and one son and draws strength and inspiration from his faith in Jesus and the power of the Holy Spirit.